14
STEPS TO
SELF-PUBLISHING
A BOOK

Mike Kowis, Esq.

14 Steps to
Self-Publishing a Book

Copyright © 2017 Mike Kowis, Esq.

www.engagingcollegestudents.com/self-publishing-guide

Library of Congress Control Number: 2017901671
ISBN-13: 978-0-9979946-5-0 (paperback)
ISBN-13: 978-0-9979946-4-3 (eBook/MOBI format)
ISBN-13: 978-0-9979946-6-7 (eBook/EPUB format)

Lecture PRO Publishing
Conroe, TX

To my beautiful wife, Jessica,

who makes me smile when I need it most.

And to our kids, Lauren and Cash,

who make me laugh out loud.

Thank you for making my life complete!

Contents

INTRODUCTION: My Self-Publishing Journey...................... 1

CHAPTER ONE: The Step-by-Step Guide...................... 3

STEP 1:   Finalize your manuscript............................ 6

STEP 2:   Create a new business to self-publish and
market your book...................................... 8

STEP 3:   Buy a domain name for your book's
website and build the webpages 10

STEP 4:   Buy ISBN numbers from Bowker 11

STEP 5:   Apply for an LCCN number from the
U.S. Library of Congress (for print books only)........ 13

STEP 6:   Apply for a merchant account at your
preferred shipping company 13

STEP 7:   Create a social media platform to promote
your book.. 14

STEP 8:   Decide where you want to sell your book
and in what formats................................. 15

STEP 9:   Hire a professional cover designer to make
your book cover 17

STEP 10: Hire a professional graphic designer to
format the interior pages of your print book
and/or convert your manuscript to an eBook............ 19

STEP 11: Purchase an editorial book review well
before the book launch date...................... 20

STEP 12: Upload your book files onto the
distributor's website..21
STEP 13: Register your book with the U.S. Copyright Office.......23
STEP 14: Market your book..23

CHAPTER TWO: Costs to Write, Self-Publish, and Market 27
CATEGORY 1: Writing Costs...29
CATEGORY 2: Self-Publishing Costs.....................................30
CATEGORY 3: Marketing Costs (for the First 90 Days)..........33

CHAPTER THREE: Ten Lessons from Writing My First Book ... 37
LESSON 1: It's a marathon.....................................38
LESSON 2: It's not cheap.......................................40
LESSON 3: Marketing is the hardest part.............................40
LESSON 4: Legal writing and book writing are different..........41
LESSON 5: Good salespeople make for successful authors........41
LESSON 6: Wise businesspeople make for successful authors........42
LESSON 7. Not everyone will buy it..................................43
LESSON 8: Book reviews are challenging.............................43
LESSON 9: Watching book sales is addictive........................44
LESSON 10: Authors help one another...............................45

CONCLUSION: If I Can Do It, Anyone Can!........................47

APPENDIX: Self-Publishing Checklist..................................49

ABOUT THE AUTHOR...55

INTRODUCTION
My Self-Publishing Journey

As a new author, the most common questions I am asked by other writers are how to self-publish a book and how much does it cost. So I decided to write this book to explain the 14 steps that I recently took to create my first book and the costs that I incurred to make it happen.

The process of self-publishing my new book—*Engaging College Students: A Fun and Edgy Guide for Professors*—in eBook, paperback, and hard cover formats took a little more than two months. I started this process in August 2016 when I received the last of two dozen rejections from traditional publishing houses to whom I had submitted my book proposal. Honestly, Plan A was that a traditional publisher would select my book for publication and take over the responsibility of turning it into a real book that I could actually hold in the palm of my hands. When that plan didn't work out, self-publishing became my only option.

Ultimately the self-publishing route worked well because I learned a ton of useful information about the book publishing process, how to create a website, and how to run a small business. Self-publishing also allowed me to maintain full control over the book's contents, interior formatting, and cover design. The best part of self-publishing is that I earn substantially more royalties from each book sale as compared to traditional publishing (e.g., self-published royalties from eBook sales can be as high as 70% as compared to only 25% for traditionally published eBook sales).

My self-publishing journey ended when my new book was officially published on October 21, 2016. Oh, what a glorious day! I felt like a proud papa when I realized that my dream of writing a book had finally become a reality after four long years of hard work.

CHAPTER ONE
The Step-by-Step Guide

For anyone interested in self-publishing a book, the good news is that the internet is overflowing with advice on how to turn a rough manuscript into a self-published book available for sale to the general public. The bad news is that the amount of guidance on this topic is overwhelming and usually spread out in pieces here and there. Many times it's hard to tell the solid, unbiased advice from that of vendors who are just pushing their services. Although I found several helpful resources on this topic (the best of which I share at the end of Chapter One), none of them captured the exact steps required to self-publish a book like mine in one concise resource. To that end, I hope this book fills that need for other writers who are interested in self-publishing their books.

Here's one last word of caution before I begin the step-by-step guide: what follows are the steps that I took to self-publish my nonfiction book in three formats (eBook, paperback, and hard cover), but these steps are not necessarily the only way or the best way. Undoubtedly there are easier or cheaper ways to self-publish. For example, you could hire a full-service vendor to do all of the steps below. That would be much easier, but more expensive than my 14-step approach. On the other hand, you could do all of the work yourself rather than outsourcing some of the work to professionals for services like copyediting, book cover design, interior formatting, photography, etc.

This option would obviously be much cheaper and could be done for a total investment of next to nothing! However, doing everything yourself would probably take more time than necessary and will most likely hurt the quality of your book (and book sales too) unless you happen to be experienced and well-skilled in those particular services.

Yet another option is to pay CreateSpace to do the professional services for you at their standard prices. The biggest downside to doing it this way is that you don't personally get to choose the vendors who perform these services nor do you have any ability to compare prices and shop around. I chose the 14 steps below because I thought they were best for my particular book, and I'm more than happy with the final product.

PRO TIP Beware of vanity presses and scam artists that promise to publish your book at egregious prices and under predatory terms. Check the internet for reviews before you hire anyone to work on your book project. For example, check out www.sfwa.org/other-resources/for-authors/writer-beware/pod.

Listed below are the 14 steps that I followed to create my first book and this book too. For your convenience, the Appendix in the back of this book includes a detailed checklist of these steps that you can refer to as you go through the process of self-publishing your next book. And though these steps worked great for my first two books, please don't feel obligated to do them all. There may be valid reasons why you may want to skip some steps. For example, if you only intend to create an eBook to be sold exclusively on Amazon, then you can probably skip steps 4 and 5 below. The right steps for your book will depend on the particular goals that you have for your book (e.g., professional quality versus low cost) and how much time and money you are willing to invest.

STEP 1: Finalize your manuscript.

STEP 2: Create a new business to self-publish and market your book.

STEP 3: Buy a domain name for your book's website and build the webpages.

STEP 4: Buy ISBN numbers from Bowker.

STEP 5: Apply for an LCCN number from the U.S. Library of Congress (for print books only).

STEP 6: Apply for a merchant account at your preferred shipping company.

STEP 7: Create a social media platform to promote your book.

STEP 8: Decide where you want to sell your book and in what formats.

STEP 9: Hire a professional cover designer to make your book cover.

STEP 10: Hire a professional graphic designer to format the interior pages of your print book and/or convert your manuscript to an eBook.

STEP 11: Purchase an editorial book review well before the book launch date.

STEP 12: Upload your book files onto the distributor's website.

STEP 13: Register your book with the U.S. Copyright Office within three months after the publication date.

STEP 14: Market your book.

Now let's walk through each step in detail and discuss how to achieve each one.

STEP 1: Finalize your manuscript. This means you should:

a. Complete your rough manuscript, including the front matter (e.g., title page, dedication, introduction, etc.) and back matter (e.g., conclusion, bibliography, acknowledgements, about the author, etc.);

b. Send it to at least three people for their review and suggested edits;

c. Have it professionally copyedited; and

d. If applicable, obtain written permission from the appropriate parties if you plan to use someone else's picture, quote, name, or likeness in your book. Sometimes written permission is not required, such as old photos available in the public domain or quotes subject to the fair use doctrine. Check with a copyright lawyer if you have any questions.

Prices vary for copyediting services depending on the editor's experience level and qualifications, but I found three cents per word was a common price when I shopped around for an experienced copyeditor to work on my first book. You could save money by hiring CreateSpace for copyediting. At the time that I published this book, they only charged one cent per word for this service and it took about two weeks to have it done. However, you don't get to choose the editor who works on your book.

Before you hire a copyeditor, make sure you are comfortable with the person's work and credentials. Some editors will let you send them a writing sample (perhaps the first chapter of your book) and they will edit it for free so you can see how good they are. Also, be sure to ask how many times you will be allowed to make revisions and send the manuscript back for another round of copyediting. In my opinion, copyediting should be a back and forth process intended to arrive at a polished product that the author is completely satisfied with. Some copyeditors only allow one round of revisions or charge more for additional rounds, while others allow unlimited rounds of revisions for no extra cost. I spent around $1,400 to have my 33,000-word manuscript copyedited and it was well worth the price! This process took three weeks, and we went through eight rounds of copyedits until I was completely satisfied with the final product.

Before you have a nonfiction book copyedited, I strongly recommend finding at least three experts related to your book's topic or who actively practice in the field to review your manuscript and provide their comments and suggested edits. This is more or less like the peer review process that traditional publishing companies use when publishing academic books. I did this step for my first book, and the comments I received from college professors were extremely helpful! The same process is also recommended for fiction books, but you should send the manuscript to serious fans of your genre so they can give their feedback based on similar fiction books they have read.

PRO TIP Skipping the professional copyediting service is a common mistake made by self-published authors that will most likely hurt the quality of the finished product and ultimately reduce book sales too. No matter how tempting it may be, don't skip this step if you want to produce a high-quality book.

<u>STEP 2:</u> **Create a new business to self-publish and market your book.** The type of business entity that you chose for your book publishing can be in any form that you prefer. I chose to set up my publishing business as a sole proprietorship because it is usually the simplest and easiest type of entity to create and run. You may want to consult with a reputable CPA or attorney to help choose the structure of your business. The process of creating a sole proprietorship can vary slightly from state to state, but these are the steps that I took to create a sole proprietorship in Texas:

a. Choose a unique name for your new business that is not the same as that of any existing business. You can search the names of existing businesses by using websites like Google and the U.S. Patent and Trademark Office. It might be wise to select a name that reflects the value or benefits of your book. For my business, I chose the name Lecture PRO Publishing because it reminds readers of the benefits that you can expect from reading my first book (i.e., you can learn to lecture college students like a "pro" if you read my book).

b. Create the legal entity. If it's a sole proprietorship, you can create it very easily. Of course, check the requirements in your state. To establish my sole proprietorship, I filed a "Doing Business As" form at my local county government's office and paid the applicable fee (less than $10). An alternative to this step was to file this form with the Secretary of State Office in my home state and pay the applicable fee ($25). NOTE: In some states you may have to publish notice of this DBA filing in certain newspapers for a minimum period of time. My state did not require this. Or you can skip all of the above and pay a vendor to handle the DBA filing for you for a service fee (approximately $100).

c. Go to the IRS website and file for an EIN number for your new business. This process is quick and easy if you choose to do it over their website. (You can file the paperwork through the mail, but it will take longer.)

d. Take the EIN number that you received from the IRS and a copy of the DBA form that you filed at the applicable government office to a bank of your choice to open a new checking account in the name of the business. NOTE: I recommend shopping around for small business checking accounts as the required minimum balance and various fees may vary significantly from bank to bank. For example, the bank I ultimately chose only requires a minimum balance of $1,500, has no monthly or annual fees provided that I maintain at least the required minimum balance in the account, and it has no monthly limit on the number of checks or transactions.

e. While you are at the bank to open the new checking account, apply for a credit card in the name of the business if you want one. With both a checking account and credit card in the name of the business, it is much easier to keep track of the business's expenses and income.

f. Another way to keep track of your new business's expenses and income is to create a spreadsheet so you can document all costs incurred and royalties received. This spreadsheet should include descriptions and dates for each expense and income item. To ensure that you capture all expenses, I recommend that you update your spreadsheet as you incur each expense or receive each income (royalty) payment rather than waiting until the end of the month to do so. I also recommend maintaining a separate (paper) file cabinet and a designated electronic file folder on your computer where you can store copies of all receipts and other important documents.

STEP 3: Buy a domain name for your book's website and build the webpages. Before you purchase a domain name, check the internet to see whether your first preference has already been taken. If your first preference is unavailable, you may consider choosing a domain name based on your author name or some other name related to your book's topic (e.g., if your nonfiction book is related to raising llamas for profit, maybe choose something on point like raisingllamas.com). I purchased my first book's website (www.engagingcollegestudents.com) from bluehost.com and paid for a three-year contract (roughly $250 depending on what extras you get).

After you have a domain name, the next step is to acquire a theme, which is the program that a website uses to arrange and display its pages. You can find a variety of themes from websites like WordPress.org. Initially I downloaded a (free) basic theme for my new website, but later upgraded it to a more advanced version by downloading a theme plug-in ($50). Other themes are more advanced than mine (e.g., contain special features or background music) and cost around $100 or more.

I learned how to buy a domain name and build a website by viewing a YouTube video that Joanna Penn created. In fact, she has created several helpful videos and articles for authors that you can find on her website (which is listed at the bottom of this article).

NOTE: Building your site's webpages is not a one-time event because you will need to continually update the pages with additional information before and after the publication date. Eventually the website should contain separate pages for the following topics:

a. About the book;
b. About the author;
c. Where the book is available for purchase and the pricing info;
d. Sample chapters or table of contents;
e. Book give-away contests, temporary price discounts, and other promotions;
f. Book reviews and paid editorial reviews; and
g. Contact information for the author.

One option to consider adding to your book's website is an invitation to sign up for your email distribution list. This works best if you offer subscribers free goodies (e.g., a helpful article you wrote or a sample chapter, or a checklist or illustration from your upcoming book) in exchange for registering their email address. Having an email list of interested readers allows you to contact them when your next book is released or when you offer a special promotion. You can build an email list using one of the many free email manager programs, such as MailChimp (www.mailchimp.com). I haven't yet added this feature to my book's website, but hope to do that soon.

STEP 4: Buy ISBN numbers from Bowker. When purchasing ISBN numbers from Bowker (www.myidentifiers.com) be sure to register using your business's name and pay the applicable fee with your business's credit card or debit card. To save money, I recommend purchasing a pack of ten ISBN numbers for $250 rather than buying them individually. You will need a separate ISBN number for each format of your book (hard cover, paperback, Kindle eBook, non-Kindle eBook, etc.) and also for any books that are translated into different languages or converted to audiobooks. I needed four ISBN numbers for my first book, so I kept the remaining six numbers for any future books that I would self-publish (including this one!).

NOTE: If you only plan to sell your book on Amazon, then you have the option of using one of CreateSpace's free ISBN numbers. This option allows you to skip this Step 4 and save a few bucks. However, there is a catch. If you use CreateSpace's free ISBN number, then CreateSpace will be listed as the official publisher of record for your book even if you set up a business entity to handle your book's publishing business pursuant to Step 2 above. Also, if you ever remove your book from CreateSpace and wish to have it published by another distributor, you will need to get a new ISBN number for your book because CreateSpace's ISBN number cannot be reassigned to another publisher. Be aware that changing the ISBN number for your book can sometimes result in confusion for consumers who may be searching for your book online using the old ISBN number. In summary, buying your own ISBN numbers for your book allows you to maintain the most control over your book and gives credit to the business you created in Step 2 as the official publisher.

PRO TIP If you live in the United States, do not purchase ISBN numbers from anyone other than Bowker. As mentioned above, ISBN numbers cannot be transferred from one publisher to another. That means a person cannot transfer their unused numbers to you. So don't be fooled by third parties offering cheap ISBN numbers for sale.

STEP 5: Apply for an LCCN number from the U.S. Library of Congress (for print books only). Follow the instructions at the U.S. Library of Congress website: www.loc.gov/publish/pcn. There is no fee to obtain this number, but you must later mail in a print copy of your book to the Library of Congress to complete the process. Once you receive your LCCN number, insert it on the title page of your book (do this Step 5 before you get the interior formatting done in Step 10 below).

NOTE: An LCCN number is usually listed on the title page of print books and does not apply to eBooks. However, having an LCCN number is not required for print books and you can skip this Step 5 if you desire. The main purpose of obtaining this number is to allow your published book to become an official part of the U.S. Library of Congress catalog of books. If you ask me, it's an honor to have my work preserved in the same book collection that contains so many famous and talented authors. Also, having this number listed on your title page makes the book look more professional in my opinion.

STEP 6: Apply for a merchant account at your preferred shipping company. Some shipping companies offer free programs that provide shipping discounts for small businesses. I registered the business that I created in Step 2 above (Lecture PRO Publishing) for the FedEx program, but I haven't actually used their discount yet because many of the review books that I shipped were mailed to post office boxes at universities, which require delivery via the U.S. Postal Service. When mailing books via U.S. Postal Service, be sure to use Media Mail delivery service for a discount. This option currently comes with free tracking and it is cheaper than both First Class service and Priority Mail service. However, Media Mail service can take up to a week for delivery depending on where the package is going. Unfortunately, I discovered Media Mail soon after I mailed 80 separate packages (containing one book each) to reviewers just prior to my book's launch date. Using the Media Mail service would have saved me 80 bucks. Ouch!

STEP 7: Create a social media platform to promote your book. This means you should spread the word about your upcoming book by creating a blog on your book's website, adding an author page to your personal Facebook account, adding your upcoming book to your LinkedIn profile, or by reaching out to the entire world via your Twitter, Pinterest, Snapchat, Goodreads, or Instagram accounts. It is not necessary to participate in all of the popular social media formats, but you need to choose at least a few formats that you feel comfortable using frequently because you should update those accounts from time to time with new information about your book. Ideally it would be best to post updates on the types of social media that are most likely to reach your target audience. For example, Facebook allows users to purchase ads that target Facebook users by gender, age, or location and LinkedIn allows users to post articles that you can share with the LinkedIn groups that you are a member of.

The main goal of creating a social media platform is to create a loyal following that will increase visibility and interest (and hopefully book sales) during and after your book launch. One effective way to create interest on your social media sites is to post pics of your final two or three book cover choices and ask folks to pick their favorite design. Another tip is to create a buzz on social media by conducting a book give-away contest as follows: Take a photo with 30 or more copies of your new book spread out all over the floor or another large surface.

A good time to do this is right after you ordered and received a large quantity of books to give away to reviewers. Then post this pic on your social media sites and ask viewers to guess the total number of books, and explain that the first person to give the correct answer will receive a free signed book. It may be wise to limit eligible contestants to U.S. residents only so that you do not end up paying to ship your book to the winner in Antarctica. I did a few of these give-away contests on my social media and they can be a lot of fun!

STEP 8: Decide where you want to sell your book and in what formats. These are important decisions because they will determine which book distributor you will use to sell your book and what type of files you need for your book. Do you want to sell a print book? If so, do you prefer paperback, hard cover, or both? Do you want to sell an eBook? If so, do you prefer Kindle, non-Kindle (e.g., Nook, Apple iBook, Kobo, etc.), or both? Do you want your book translated into foreign languages or made into an audiobook? Do you want to sell your book on a single website with high traffic, like Amazon, or do you want broader availability so that your readers can find you in several places, including libraries?

The bottom line is that there are currently several print-on-demand book distributors that will gladly sell your self-published book, including CreateSpace (which distributes paperback books to Amazon plus its extended distribution channels), KDP (distributes Kindle eBooks to Amazon only), Ingram Spark (distributes paperback, hard cover, and non-Kindle eBooks to approximately 30,000 book retailers worldwide, including BarnesandNoble.com), and a host of other distributors.

NOTE: Just prior to this book's publication, KDP announced that it will begin distributing paperback books to be sold on Amazon. So that is another option to be aware of. Choosing to sell your book on Amazon is a popular choice because their website currently sells more print and eBooks than any other book retailer in the world.

For my first book I chose CreateSpace and KDP to distribute my paperback and Kindle eBook, respectively, on Amazon. I also chose Ingram Spark so I could sell my book in hard cover format on Amazon. Ingram Spark also sells my hard cover, paperback, and non-Kindle books to a wide variety of book retailers around the world. For the book you're reading now, I chose CreateSpace and KDP to distribute my paperback and Kindle eBook, respectively, on Amazon. To save money, I did not opt to distribute the print version of this book through Ingram Spark. The downsides of skipping Ingram Spark are that this book is not offered in hard cover and many bookstores will not carry this book on their shelves because they prefer to order books for resale from distributors like Ingram Spark rather than a big competitor such as Amazon (which owns CreateSpace and KDP).

There are pros and cons for each print-on-demand distributor, so do your research and choose the distributor that is right for your particular book. Some distributors offer choices that require exclusivity. For example, if you choose KDP to distribute your Kindle eBook on Amazon, you have the option of joining the KDP Select, which will make your book available to more readers. However, this option requires your eBook to be exclusively offered for sale through KDP and you cannot sell your non-Kindle eBook via other outlets (such as BarnesandNoble.com or kobo.com). For this reason, I elected out of the KDP Select option.

Once you decide which book distributor(s) that you want to use, you need to register for an account on their website(s) using your business name as the official publisher of your book and using your business' checking or credit card account to pay any applicable fees (e.g., to purchase review copies) and to receive royalty payments.

PRO TIP You can also choose to sell your book directly from your book's website. However, be aware that you may have to collect payments from your customers and remit sales taxes to the applicable state taxing authorities. I didn't want to mess with this or the possibility of making frequent trips to the post office to ship the books, so I decided to skip this option.

STEP 9: Hire a professional cover designer to make your book cover. Hiring a talented cover designer is probably the most important decision you can make as a self-publisher because the cover is the first thing readers will see and they will usually be able to tell immediately whether the book cover has been designed professionally or by an amateur. If your book cover grabs the reader's eye and appears interesting and professional, there is at least a decent chance that folks will buy it. If the front cover is crap, no one will buy it except your mom. Period.

There are several book cover designers offering their services on the internet with prices ranging from dirt cheap to a thousand bucks or more, but most have prices in the $100 to $400 range. At the time of this book's publication, CreateSpace offered this service for $399 and the process usually takes around two to four weeks. The eBook cover is the simplest cover to make because it only contains the front page image (usually saved as a JPG file), whereas the cover for print books will include a front page, spine and back page (usually saved as a PDF file). Many cover designers charge a combo price for doing an eBook cover plus one print book (either a paperback or hard cover). The designer that I hired (Derek Murphy from CreativINDIE Covers) for my first book charged a little less than $850, but that price included covers for my eBook, paperback, and hard cover. I also received a few pics to promote my book on the book's website and through social media. To save money on the book you are reading now, I hired a different book designer who charged around $300. Ultimately I was willing pay more for the book cover designer that I hired for my first book because this person did excellent work for other books in my genre, had lots of experience, and came highly recommended by other authors who had used him previously. I expected him to do an excellent job on my cover, and (in my humble opinion) I was right. Thanks, Derek!

To find the right cover designer for your book, I recommend searching other books in your genre to get an idea of what features and design ideas you want to incorporate into your cover. Then search for a reputable book cover designer with experience making covers in your genre. Many book cover designers have websites displaying examples of their previous work. Pay particular attention to any covers that stand out and may appeal to your target audience.

If you need a cover made for print books you will need the following items for the back cover:

a. Sales description of the book (briefly explain what it's about and why readers should buy it);
b. Short description of the author and his/her credentials;
c. Author photo (a professional headshot is recommended if you can afford it);
d. Your book's website address;
e. The publisher's name (the business you created in Step 2 above);

   f.   The ISBN number and its barcode (the book cover designer should be able to supply the barcode, but if not there are many free ISBN barcode generators online); and

   g.   Blurbs (optional quotes from famous or influential people who praise the book in their own words).

PRO TIP Unless you are already an experienced and skilled graphic designer, I don't recommend designing your own book cover as this is a common rookie mistake. It will usually be obvious to most readers that your cover does not look professional and many readers may instantly be turned off. Also, I don't recommend adding pricing information on the back cover because you will need to revise the cover and upload the revised book cover files to your distributor if you later decide to change the suggested retail price of your print book.

STEP 10: **Hire a professional graphic designer to format the interior pages of your print book and/or convert your manuscript to an eBook.** Again, shop around for these services as they can vary greatly in price and quality. Many vendors charge a few hundred bucks for this service. At the time of this book's publication, CreateSpace charged approximately $250 to $375 for its interior formatting service and about $80 for conversion to Kindle eBook. Their interior formatting service usually takes two to four weeks to be completed.

I paid about $400 to hire the graphic designer for my first book. That price included formatting the interior pages of my print books and converting them to a PDF file (the same PDF file will work for both the paperback and hard cover) as well as converting my manuscript document into two types of eBook files (a Mobi file for Kindle eBooks and an Epub file for non-Kindle eBooks). For the book you are reading now, I hired a different graphic designer who charged only $100 for the same services. Be aware that if you later decide to make small revisions to the interior pages of your print or eBook (e.g., to correct typos), then you may have to pay your book designer additional fees for the revisions to the applicable files. Also, some distributors (such as Ingram Spark) may require you to pay additional fees to upload the revised PDF and eBook files to the distributor's website.

NOTE: It's possible to skip this Step 10 and create a PDF directly from Microsoft Word (this option, oddly, is part of the Print menu) or either a PDF or an Epub file directly from Apple Pages. Publishing houses use Adobe InDesign to create the final pages that they send to their printers, and as of this writing that application was available for just $19.99 per month. But just as I advised against designing your own cover unless you're a skilled graphic designer, the same goes for the interior of your book. Page layout requires a lot more than just setting margins—crafting an attractive font palette is also something that's best left to the experts.

PRO TIP Be aware that some fonts require an additional fee for commercial usage on your book's cover or interior pages, and that fee may or may not be included in the standard price charged by your book cover designer or graphic designer. For example, I paid about $40 to use a special font in my first book's interior because my graphic designer did not already have a commercial license to use that particular font.

STEP 11: Purchase an editorial book review well before the book launch date. You can add a purchased editorial book review to the book's listing (on Amazon and other websites) to praise the book's virtues from a third party's point of view. A positive editorial review can be especially helpful when your book is first launched and typically has few or no book reviews from readers. Keep in mind that some paid reviewers require the book to be submitted for review at least two or three months before the publication date.

The top of the line book reviewers (e.g., Clarion and Kirkus) charge around $400 to $600 depending on how fast you need it, whereas the smaller book review companies charge around $100 (give or take) and offer faster service. I paid only $60 for my first book's editorial review by Don Sloan of PublishersDailyReviews.com and it was completed in only a few days. His review was excellent and well-worth the small investment. Of course, just because the book review costs money doesn't mean it will automatically be a favorable review. The paid reviewer will usually let you review a draft of the book review before it's published and let you decide whether the review should be published or not.

STEP 12: Upload your book files onto the distributor's website.
Follow the instructions on the website of the distributor(s) that you chose for your book. For CreateSpace, you need to upload the interior PDF file and the paperback cover file. For KDP, you need to upload the Mobi file and eBook cover file. For Ingram Spark, you need to upload several files, including the interior PDF file (the same PDF works for both paperback and hard cover), plus the two print cover files (one for the paperback and another one for the hard cover) as well as the Epub file and eBook cover file.

Be prepared to enter the following information when you upload your book files:

a. The title and subtitle of your book;

b. The name(s) of the author(s) and illustrator(s) of your book;

c. The publisher's name (the business you created in Step 2 above);

d. For print books, the trim size (e.g., 6" x 9");

e. The sales description of the book;

f. Two or three BISAC codes that best fit the categories of your book (see http://bisg.org/page/BISACSubjectCodes);

g. The ISBN numbers assigned to each version of your book; and

h. Five to seven keywords or short phrases that best describe your book. (Think of these as search terms that readers are most likely to enter into Amazon or BarnesandNoble.com to find a book like yours.)

NOTE: When I uploaded my book's files, there was no fee for uploading files onto CreateSpace and KDP. Ingram Spark usually charges a one-time fee to upload book files. However, my first book's upload fees were waived because I took advantage of a promotion that Ingram Spark offered at that time. Ingram Spark usually charges a small annual fee to continue selling your book through its distribution channels, but so far as I'm aware, CreateSpace and KDP do not. Of course, the business model of these book distributors may change at any time, so please double check the terms and conditions of your chosen book distributor before registering and uploading your book files.

PRO TIP Choosing the right keywords is crucial for helping potential buyers find your book on the seller's website, so choose them wisely. You can and should revise these keywords later if you discover better words or phrases for your book. (See Step 14 below.)

STEP 13: Register your book with the U.S. Copyright Office. Within three months of your book's publication date, register your book with the U.S. Copyright Office. To do so, simply follow the instructions for the online registration form on the eCO Registration System (https://copyright.gov/registration). You must also pay the applicable fee ($35) and mail two copies of your book to the U.S. Library of Congress after publication to complete the process. Total processing time can take up to nine months for an electronic filing and up to twice that time for a paper filing.

NOTE: Mailing two copies to complete your U.S. copyright registration does not satisfy the requirement to mail in one copy to complete the LCCN process described in Step 5 above.

STEP 14: Market your book. Ask any published author and they will readily tell you that marketing is the hardest step! This work is endless, complex, and can easily soak up every dollar and every spare minute that you are willing to invest. For those reasons, a detailed discussion of this Step 14 is beyond the scope of this book. However, I will mention some of the marketing efforts that I used to promote my first book during its first 90 days, including:

a. Announcing the book launch date well in advance via your social media platform to drive up interest (and hopefully sales) when it first hits the market and also to promote pre-orders (if your book distributor accepts pre-orders);

b. If you are selling your book on Amazon, creating a free author page on Amazon's Author Central website to help potential buyers learn more about you (the author) and promote your book's website;

c. If you are selling your Kindle eBook on Amazon via KDP, purchasing click-through ads from the Amazon Marketing Service using up to 1,000 keywords or short phrases that you select for your book. As the click-through ads run on Amazon, your KDP website (dashboard page) will display the ad results for each selected keyword, including how many times your ad was displayed, how many times the ad resulted in a click, and how many clicks resulted in a purchased book. This advertising data reveals the optimal keywords to help potential buyers find your book. With this information, you should revise the original five to seven keywords that you entered on your distributor's website when you uploaded the book files. You can also purchase or post free ads on your Facebook author page, LinkedIn page, Goodreads.com, and other social media pages. In the first two months following the launch date of my first book, almost half of all book sales came from the Amazon Marketing Service click-through ads that I purchased. After the first two months, these ads stopped having such a big impact on my sales and I decided to switch to other marketing efforts. I might try these ads again in the future. NOTE: you must distribute your Kindle eBook via KDP to be eligible to purchase these Amazon ads;

d. Giving free review copies to friends, family, and other interested parties and asking them to consider leaving an honest review on Amazon if they enjoy reading your book. The reality is that many folks who receive a free book are more likely to leave a favorable review than an unfavorable review. In my experience, only a small portion (about one-quarter) of the total review copies you give away will result in actual book reviews simply because many folks lead busy lives and may never get around to reading your book and leaving a review;

e. Participating in book give-away contests on Goodreads.com. Be sure to register as a new member on the Goodreads website and claim your author profile and book at least a few weeks in advance of the planned book give-away to allow time for approvals by Goodreads staff. Also, post your book give-away contests on your book's website to drive traffic there; and

f. Entering your book in reputable book contests to build credibility with readers if your book is chosen for an award or honorable mention. Caution: Book contests have mixed reviews and some folks say these contests are nothing more than a profit center, especially if they charge high entry fees and do not provide substantial prizes to the winners. Also, unknown book contests often provide little or no prestige for the winners. Check the reviews of book contests before you enter, and see http://selfpublishingadvice.org/allis-self-publishing-service-directory/award-and-contest-ratings-reviews for more information.

Before you attempt to implement any of the above steps, I **strongly recommend** that all first-time book authors read the following three resources:

a. *The Essential Guide to Getting Your Book Published: How to Write It, Sell It, and Market It . . . Successfully* by Arielle Eckstut and David H. Sterry. This thorough book provides an excellent overview of the book publishing business and offers practical advice to authors who desire to self-publish or go through the traditional publishing route. It also covers other important topics such how to market your book, which is useful to all authors regardless of how you publish your book.

b. *Self-Publisher's Legal Handbook: The Step-by-Step Guide to the Legal Issues of Self-Publishing* by Helen Sedwick. This practical handbook is a must read for any author interested in self-publishing because it provides many useful tips, such as how to set up a new business to create and sell your book, how to obtain ISBN numbers, what copyright protections apply, and how to avoid infringing the copyright of others, etc.

c. The Creative Penn blog (www.thecreativepenn.com) by Joanna Penn. This website offers tons of free advice for new authors, including articles, podcasts, and YouTube vids to show authors how to write a book manuscript, self-publish their print or eBook, and market their book after it's published. As stated above, I used one of Joanna's YouTube vids to learn how to buy a domain name and build the webpage for my book's website, www.engagingcollegestudents.com. With Joanna's sage advice, this task was much easier than I had imagined.

CHAPTER TWO
Costs to Write, Self-Publish, and Market

When I began writing my first book a little more than four years ago, I never stopped to consider how much it would cost to produce the final product, bring it to market, and then spread the word to potential customers. I simply started typing and assumed the cost would be minimal. Fast forward to today (approximately four months after I published *Engaging College Students: A Fun and Edgy Guide for Professors*), and the reality of just how expensive this endeavor actually was has finally sunk in. To date, I have spent a GRAND TOTAL of approximately ...

[*drum roll please*]

Seven thousand smack-a-roos! Really? Really, really? Holy Toledo! Where did all that money go?

For anyone thinking about self-publishing your future book, you might be interested in the following breakdown of the costs to write, self-publish, and market my first book in three formats (eBook, paperback, and hard cover) via CreateSpace, KDP, and Ingram Spark. Of course, there are plenty of other self-published books created and promoted for much less than my first book and others that cost quite a bit more, and how much you are willing to spend on your book is up to you. In fact, I set a much lower budget for this book, as explained below. So please don't think that the investment I made on my first book is necessarily what's best for yours.

When planning what I would be willing to spend on my first book, I made a firm decision to focus on the quality of my book rather than being cost-conscious and efficient. Top quality was of utmost importance for my first book because most of my first book's competitors were traditionally published and professionally designed. The main goal for my first book was to look as professional as its competition and be able to compete well against them.

On the other hand, my primary goal for this book was to self-publish it as cost effectively as possible while still maintaining high quality by following my 14-step approach. Unlike my first book, which took four years and a whopping $7,000 to create, self-publish, and market for its first 90 days, this book took only two months and approximately $1,500. The point is that every book's self-publishing journey is different in terms of the optimal amount of time and financial investment. However, I recommend that you follow the same 14-step process for every book that you write to increase your book's chance of success.

In any case, the following cost breakdown for my first and second books should give others a rough idea of what to expect if they decide to take a similar path down the exciting road of Self-Publishing Avenue.

CATEGORY 1: Writing Costs

First Book = $2,400*

Developmental Edits... $1,000
Copyediting... $1,400

DETAILS: I hired a freelance editor—not once, but twice — for developmental edits ($500 each) to cure two separate bouts of writer's block. When I say that I struggled with writer's block two times, I mean they were *terminal* cases with zero hope to write another page. Each time this happened, I turned to my muse and freelance book editor (Mr. Geoff Smith of Brooklyn, NY) to provide fresh ideas for additional topics. These developmental edits were a life saver for my book. Most writers can probably skip the developmental editing unless you get totally stuck like I did. On the other hand, copyediting your final manuscript is absolutely necessary for self-published authors if your goal is to produce a professional product that sells.

This Book = $400*

Copyediting... $400 (this cost was less expensive than my first book because of the significantly lower word count)

DETAILS: To gauge public interest in this book, I wrote three articles about my first book's self-publishing journey and published them on my website. These articles were well-received on my social media platform and many readers encouraged me to write a book on this topic. So I combined these articles and made them into the rough manuscript for this book and hired Geoff to once again work his copyediting magic.

*NOTE: The above writing costs exclude the purchase of a personal computer and writing software (e.g., Microsoft Word, Scrivener, or Adobe InDesign) because I already had these necessary tools of the trade.

CATEGORY 2: Self-Publishing Costs

First Book = $2,500

Domain name, webhosting contract (three years), and website theme... $300

ISBN numbers (pack of ten)... $250

Book cover design... $850

Interior formatting and eBook conversion, including later corrections for typos... $500

Professional author pic (for back cover, website, social media pages, etc.)... $150

Purchased rights to use names, likenesses, and quotes of third parties used in the book... $100

Editorial book review... $100

Proof copies of print books and fast shipping from Ingram Spark/CreateSpace... $100

File uploading fees for Ingram Spark (CreateSpace was free)... $100

Registration with the U.S. Copyright Office, including cost to mail two copies… $50

DETAILS: The cost to obtain and build a website for your book is a must for all authors regardless of whether your book is self-published or published by a traditional publishing house. However, you can save a little money by finding free themes (webpage designs) on sites like WordPress.org. As I stated in Chapter One, I started with a free theme but later added a $50 plug-in to make my website look a little more professional.

Like the professional copyediting service recommended above, I also highly recommend getting your book cover made by a professional. Despite the old saying, most people do judge a book by its cover, and they'll look right past your book if the cover looks unprofessional or unappealing. As a side benefit, you can create interest in your upcoming book by posting a few alternative book cover designs on your social media pages and asking the public to vote for their favorite design.

Getting a paid editorial book review is also a good idea for several reasons. For starters, you can list your favorite quotes from the editorial review in your online listing for Amazon, Barnes and Noble, and other websites. Second, a paid editorial book review can be useful for catching any remaining typos that your copyeditor didn't find. Don Sloan gave an excellent editorial review of my book and also found eight typos/missing words. Of course I immediately paid to revise my interior book files and eBook files to correct these errors so that all future books are perfect (or as close as possible).

Instead of buying just one ISBN number, I bought a pack of ten because I needed a different number for each format of my book (one for the Kindle eBook sold through KDP Amazon, one for the non-Kindle eBook sold through Ingram Spark, one for the paperback sold via CreateSpace and Ingram Spark, and one for the hard cover sold through Ingram Spark and Amazon). As I mentioned above in Chapter One, I can use the remaining six numbers for future books that I self-publish (including this one).

This Book = $600

Book cover design... $300

Interior formatting and eBook conversion... $100

Editorial book review... $100

Proof copies of print books and fast shipping from CreateSpace... $50

Registration with the U.S. Copyright Office, including cost to mail two copies... $50

DETAILS: To save money on this book, I selected less expensive vendors for the cover design, interior formatting, and eBook conversion. I also reused my author photo from my first book, and I didn't need to purchase ISBN numbers because I had plenty left over from the original pack of ten. I've also been able to write about this book on my first book's website instead of buying a new domain name and creating a new one. Using the same site for both books saved money, but it may make it a little harder for my readers to find the webpages for this book. If you plan to write more than one book, the simplest and most effective approach may be to create a single author website that contains information about all of your books.

CATEGORY 3: Marketing Costs (for the First 90 Days)

First book = $2,100

Purchased 150 paperback copies and mailed them to colleges, news media, give-away contest winners, and book reviewers... $1,050

Entered ten book contests... $800

Ads on Facebook, Amazon, and Goodreads... $150

Office supplies (envelopes and postage) to mail books and follow-up letters... $100

DETAILS: There are many different ways to promote your new book, and every author has his or her own strategy for doing that. For whatever reason, strategies that seem to work well for one book have zero impact on another. My marketing strategy was to try several different activities and see what worked well for my book.

This book = $500 (estimate)

Purchasing 30 paperback copies and mailing them to give-away contest winners and book reviewers... $200

Entering two book contests... $150

Purchasing ads on Facebook, Amazon, and Goodreads... $150

DETAILS: To save money, I will be more selective with my marketing campaigns for this book. However, I feel that it's critical to focus on getting honest book reviews on Amazon as soon as possible and then maintaining an active presence on my social media platform.

To promote the launch of my first book, I mainly focused on four activities. First, I purchased several books just before the launch date and mailed them to colleges in my area (potential customers), news media (this was a stab in the dark because I don't have any personal contacts in that industry), and book reviewers (my colleagues, former students, friends, and family) along with a personal note asking each recipient to please consider leaving an honest review online if they enjoyed my new book.

Second, I participated in multiple book give-away contests on Goodreads and through my social media pages and posted links to these give-away contests on my book's webpage.

Third, I purchased sponsored ads for my book on Facebook as well as click-through ads on Amazon and Goodreads.

Fourth, I entered ten book contests. Admittedly, entering so many book contests was not cheap and many folks have differing opinions as to how effective these contests can be. My thoughts were that entering several book contests would increase my odds of winning at least one contest and thereafter I could advertise my book as an "award-winning book" (for whatever that is worth). More important, many book contests provide publicity for their winners via various websites and award ceremonies. A few contests offer cash prizes and free book promotion services to the winners. And as a previously unknown author, I believe there is at least some value if a third party recognizes and praises my writing chops even if that third party happens to be a book contest organization. Happily, my gamble paid off and my debut book recently won its first book contest. It was selected as the solo Medalist Winner in the Education category of the 2016 New Apple Annual Book Awards for Excellence in Independent Publishing. There is no cash prize with this particular award, but it feels great to have some validation of my writing chops. More important, this award should result in some much-needed publicity and hopefully a bump in book sales too.

I also pursued other marketing strategies for my first book, but I'll cover those in a future article on my book's website.

CHAPTER THREE
Ten Lessons from Writing My First Book

Writing and self-publishing my first book took four long years and countless hours of staring at a computer screen. Alas, my hard work is not yet done as I continue to try a variety of marketing activities to promote my book. I'm happy to report it was well worth the time and effort it took to produce my award-winning debut book, *Engaging College Students: A Fun and Edgy Guide for Professors.* In addition to learning about the book creation process, I discovered a lot about myself and others. Below are the top ten pearls of wisdom that I gathered from this challenging but rewarding experience.

LESSON 1: It's a marathon.

LESSON 2: It's not cheap.

LESSON 3: Marketing is the hardest part.

LESSON 4: Legal writing and book writing are different.

LESSON 5: Good salespeople make for successful authors.

LESSON 6: Wise businesspeople make for successful authors.

LESSON 7: Not everyone will buy it.

LESSON 8: Book reviews are challenging.

LESSON 9: Watching book sales is addictive.

LESSON 10: Authors help one another.

Now let's discuss each one in detail.

LESSON 1: **It's a marathon.** Writing, self-publishing, and marketing a book takes much more time than I ever imagined. When I set out to write a book, it took me about 18 months just to pick a topic. After much soul searching, I concluded that I should pick a topic that I felt genuinely passionate about. Eventually I realized that my (part-time) college teaching career and the lessons I learned therefrom fit that criteria perfectly. With the topic selected, I publicly announced to friends and family that I would complete my first book within a year. Looking back, that was a very ambitious goal for someone with a full-time career, a part-time teaching job, and a family to raise. Before I knew it, one year turned into two, then three and by the end of year four I finally finished and self-published my new book. What a long and interesting journey!

Below is a complete timeline of my first book's four-year process.

Spring 2011: I decided to write a book, but was unsure of the topic. (hmmm …)

November 7, 2012: I decided to write about my college teaching experiences because I was passionate about teaching and wanted to share the lessons I had learned during my college teaching career. To motivate myself to follow through on this goal, I publicly announced on Facebook that I was writing a book and it would be complete in less than a year. (Can you say "wishful thinking"? Ha!)

Here is my actual Facebook post:

"[Mike Kowis] is WRITING A BOOK about teaching based on my experiences teaching night classes at the local community college during the past 10+ years. It took me a whole year to select a topic to write about, so I'm truly excited to finally begin this book … hope to finish it by Labor Day 2013. So far, I have drafted the first 10 pages (including the outline). I just hope I can see it through to the end b/c I've wanted to write a book for many years. Wish me luck!"

November 2013: Only 57 pages done. Say what? I was a little embarrassed that I failed to meet my one-year goal, but I pressed on. (You can do it!)

November 2014: 80 pages done and then I came down with a bad case of writer's block. So I enlisted the help of freelance editor Geoff Smith. Geoff provided some much-needed developmental edits, and soon I was off and running again. (Geoff to the rescue!)

November 2015: 113 pages done, but writer's block struck again! So I went back to Geoff for more developmental edits. (Thanks again, Geoff!)

May 2016: 160 pages done and the rough draft of the manuscript was finally finished! (Can I get an amen?)

June 2016: I asked four college professors to review my rough manuscript and give their feedback. (Thank you!)

July 2016: I hired Geoff for copyediting and then exchanged eight rounds of edits to polish up the manuscript. (Geoff is the best!)

August 2016: I completed the final book manuscript—hallelujah! I also created the book's website (www.engagingcollegestudents.com) and established a social media presence on Facebook (author page), LinkedIn groups, Goodreads, etc.

September 2016: I hired Derek Murphy from CreativINDIE Covers for the book cover design (Great job, Derek!) and another vendor for the interior formatting and eBook conversion.

October 21, 2016: This was the official publication date of my first book and the date it finally became available for sale on Amazon. NOTE: I publicized November 1 as the launch date to ensure that my book would actually be available on multiple websites by that date. This was necessary because I didn't know exactly when my book would be available for retailers that purchase my book through Ingram Spark.

November 1, 2016: This was the publicized book launch date for my book. (Whoo hoo!)

LESSON 2: **It's not cheap.** Writing, self-publishing, and marketing a *quality* book can be pricey. As stated above, I have spent about seven grand to create and market my first book, and I think this amount is a bit high compared to other self-published books. No doubt, recouping my financial investment and someday earning a profit on my book is a daunting challenge for a brand-new author like me. If someone had told me before I started this process that I'd spend that much $$$ to make my first book a reality, I probably would have pooped my pants, called that person a liar, or both. But honestly, you can't put a price on a person's life goal, and I'm so glad that I finally wrote and published my first book (and would be even if I hadn't sold a single copy).

LESSON 3: **Marketing is the hardest part.** Talk about naïve! When I started writing my first book, I didn't have a clue how my book would eventually be published and promoted. I just assumed that all books are listed on sites like Amazon and they sell themselves. Writing and self-publishing my book were hard at times, but marketing my book has been by far the hardest part of the process. This is probably because I had full control over the writing and self-publishing processes, but zero control over someone else's decision to buy my book. All I can do to influence book sales is spread the word about my "must-read" book through word of mouth, social media, book give-away contests, advertising campaigns, and other promotions. Also, the fact that I am not a natural-born salesman doesn't help (this is probably typical for many authors).

LESSON 4: **Legal writing and book writing are different.** After two decades of practicing tax law, I consider myself to be a fairly competent writer. Sloppy legal writing can have dire consequences, especially when drafting a contract or legal opinion involving a multimillion-dollar transaction. It's critical for lawyers like myself to draft precise language that is often repetitive, tedious to read, and overly detailed (leaving nothing to the imagination of the reader). Write a book in that style and the reader will fall asleep before the end of page two. While drafting and editing my rough manuscript, I discovered that my daily writing style was too technical and boring for book writing purposes. With the help of my talented editor, Geoff Smith, I learned how to write prose in a more natural style and allow my readers to make natural assumptions from my writings. This resulted in a more free-flowing style that was much more fun to read.

LESSON 5: **Good salespeople make for successful authors.** After I finished writing my manuscript, I was faced with the choice of either: 1) pitching my book to book agents (who in turn can pitch your book to their contacts at traditional publishing houses), 2) pitching my book directly to traditional publishing companies, or 3) self-publishing my book and then pitching my book to potential readers. Obviously all three alternatives require the author to be a good salesperson.

Initially I decided to take option #2 above and submitted three-dozen book proposals to traditional publishing companies that publish books in the higher education genre. To my dismay, writing a book proposal is much more involved than putting together a simple book report like students do in high school. Creating an effective book proposal requires researching the book's target market and competitors as well as the persuasive touch of a good salesperson. Specifically, the proposal must describe the need for a book like yours and how your book fills that need, the target audience of your book, and an explanation of how your book is distinguishable from its competitors currently on the market. The book proposal must also include a marketing plan and plans for creating a social media platform. Despite my best efforts, none of the traditional publishing companies that I pursued were willing to take a chance on my new book. So I decided to pursue option #3 above and self-publish it. That means I am now responsible for all of the book marketing activities—whether I want to be a salesman or not.

<u>LESSON 6</u>: **Wise businesspeople make for successful authors.** At its core, a published author is a business owner. You have created a product that you intend to sell to the public, either directly as a self-publisher or indirectly via a traditional publishing house. Like any business owner, published authors must make wise spending decisions, keep track of their competitors, record all expenses and royalty income, and be willing to hire outside vendors when necessary. One thing I learned is that authors who self-publish their books should consider creating a separate business entity to be the

official publisher of the book, and that business should have its own bank account and debit card/credit card to keep track of the money flowing in and out of the book business. As explained in Chapter One, I did this by creating a sole proprietorship and it was surprisingly easy to do.

LESSON 7. Not everyone will buy it. If I tell someone about my new book and they cheerfully promise to buy a copy, that doesn't mean they will actually buy it. When this first happened to me, I got all giddy inside with the prospect of having a sale and hopefully a new fan of my work. Keep in mind that book sales were very slow for my book during the first few weeks. When I checked my sales numbers to see if I could figure out whether that person bought one of my eBooks, paperbacks, or hard covers, I soon realized that no one had bought my book that day or within the next several days. Bummer! I had gotten all excited for nothing. After the same thing happened a few more times, I realized that those folks mean well, but don't always follow through with what they say. Personally, I'd rather they just say congrats or say nothing at all. In any case, I don't take it personally if someone doesn't buy my book. My book is not intended for everyone, and I shouldn't expect everyone to buy it (including the folks who say they will).

LESSON 8: Book reviews are challenging. To my chagrin, it's not easy to get online book reviews even if you give away several free books to friends, family, and other acquaintances. This was a particularly difficult lesson for me because I had imagined that all of my friends, family, coworkers, and former students would eagerly read my new book and quickly leave an honest book review online, especially if I gave them a free copy. Though many of them promised they would read my book and leave a review, the reality is that less than 25% actually have so far. (I'm still hoping at least a few more will do so in the near future.)

In hindsight this should not have been a big surprise. After all, I'm way more excited about my first book than anyone else and rightfully so. I have invested four years of my life and thousands of dollars into this book, whereas my family and other acquaintances have not. More important, many of them have busy lives/careers/family obligations, and reading my silly book is not a high priority (nor should it be). Even though my book contains humor that should appeal to most any adult, the reality is that my first book has a narrow target audience (college professors or anyone who trains adults), and most of my friends and family are not within this target audience. In addition, some folks are not familiar with online book sites like Amazon or simply don't feel comfortable writing a book review. In any case, I don't regret giving away so many free books to those whom I love and admire. I just wish that I had lowered my expectations as to how many folks would actually take the time to read my book and leave a review.

LESSON 9: Watching book sales is addictive. Even though it has been four months since I published my first book, I still get excited whenever I check my online "dashboard" (the book distributor's website that displays the author's latest total book sales and royalties) to see whether I sold any books that day. For better or worse, I seem to unconsciously allow the recent number of sales to dictate my mood.

Only a few months after my book launch, I sold eight books in one day—a new personal record—and I was on cloud nine all weekend! But the following week I went three straight days without a single sale, and that demoralized me a bit. As time goes on, I'm sure the thrill of checking my daily sales numbers will eventually wear off, and I will finally stop using sales data as a form of self-validation. For the sake of my sanity, I hope that happens soon!

<u>LESSON 10</u>: **Authors help one another.** One pleasant surprise for me was how generous established authors are with their time and advice to help other authors. Just to name a few, established authors Joanna Penn and Derek Murphy offer tons of free advice for aspiring authors on their websites, www.thecreativepenn.com and www.creativindie.com, respectively. After I hired Derek Murphy to create my first book's cover, I discovered that he often speaks at writing conferences and offers free books with practical advice for authors-to-be. There are also countless blogs, forums, Facebook groups, LinkedIn groups, and other online communities that are filled with published authors freely giving their time to answer questions and give advice to anyone who asks. If you get stuck or have questions on your writing journey, I strongly encourage you to reach out for help from other authors who have already gone down the path you're seeking. Helpful advice is available in spades and often it's free.

CONCLUSION
If I Can Do It, Anyone Can!

To summarize, simply follow the 14 steps above and you should be able to self-publish your tome in about one to two months. Just be sure to bring your wallet along because this journey ain't cheap. By following my 14-step approach, you should expect to spend between $1,500 and $7,000 to create, self-publish, and market your professional-looking book through its first 90 days.

If you're like me, your book launch date will be a deeply rewarding and happy occasion. At that point in your journey, you have joined an exclusive group of people who can call themselves a published author. It may sound kinda funny at first, but you will get used to being called a published author and rightfully so—you earned it! However, that day also marks the beginning of the hardest part of the journey. Marketing your book is a never-ending battle and finding what promotional activities work best for your particular book can be the most challenging part of being an author.

Here's the bottom line. If I can do it, anyone can. Good luck with your upcoming book!

APPENDIX
Self-Publishing Checklist

❑ <u>STEP 1: Finalize your manuscript.</u>

    a. Complete your rough manuscript, including the front matter and back matter;

    b. Send it to at least three people for their review and suggested edits;

    c. Have it professionally copyedited; and

    d. If applicable, obtain written permission from the appropriate parties if you plan to use someone else's picture, quote, name, or likeness in your book.

❑ <u>STEP 2: Create a new business to self-publish and market your book.</u>

    a. Choose a unique name for your new business that is not the same as that of any existing business;

    b. Create the legal entity;

    c. Go to the IRS website and file for an EIN number for your new business;

    d. Take the EIN number that you received from the IRS and a copy of the DBA form that you filed at the applicable government office to a bank of your choice to open a new checking account in the name of the business; and

e. While you are at the bank to open the new checking account, apply for a credit card in the name of the business if you want one.

❑ STEP 3: Buy a domain name for your book's website and build the webpages.

a. If you don't know how to do this step, check out the YouTube video that Joanna Penn created on this topic; and

b. Be sure to include the following information on the website:

- About the book,
- About the author,
- Where the book is available for purchase and the pricing information,
- Sample chapters or table of contents,
- Book give-away contests, temporary price discounts, and other promotions,
- Book reviews and paid editorial reviews, and
- Contact information for the author.

❑ STEP 4: Buy ISBN numbers. When purchasing ISBN numbers from Bowker (www.myidentifiers.com), be sure to register using your business's name and pay the applicable fee ($250 for ten numbers) with your business's credit card or debit card.

❑ STEP 5: Apply for an LCCN number from the U.S. Library of Congress (for print books only). Follow the instructions at the U.S. Library of Congress website. Be sure to mail in a print copy of your book to the Library of Congress to complete the process. Once you receive your LCCN number, insert it on the title page of your book.

❏ STEP 6: Apply for a merchant account at your preferred shipping company. You should consider signing up for the FedEx program if you think their shipping discount could save you money.

❏ STEP 7: Create a social media platform to promote your book. You should spread the word about your upcoming book by:

    a. Creating a blog on your book's website;

    b. Adding an author page to your personal Facebook account;

    c. Adding your upcoming book to your LinkedIn profile; and

    d. Reaching out to the entire world via your Twitter, Pinterest, Snapchat, Goodreads, and/or Instagram accounts.

❏ STEP 8: Decide where you want to sell your book and in what formats. Format options include eBooks, paperbacks, and hard covers. Popular distributors for self-publishers include CreateSpace, KDP, Ingram Spark, and several others.

❏ STEP 9: Hire a professional cover designer to make your book cover. For print books only, you will need the following information to make the back cover:

    a. Sales description of the book;

    b. A short author bio with your credentials;

    c. Your author photo;

    d. Your book's website address;

    e. The publisher's name;

    f. The ISBN number and its barcode; and

    g. Blurbs from writers or experts in your field.

❏ STEP 10: Hire a professional graphic designer to format the interior pages of your print book and/or convert your manuscript to an eBook.

❏ STEP 11: Purchase an editorial book review. Popular vendors include Clarion, Kirkus, and Publishers Daily Reviews.

❏ STEP 12: Upload your book files onto the distributor's website. The types of book files you will need depends on the format of the book(s) and which distributor you select:

    a. For Kindle eBooks distributed on Amazon via KDP, you will need the eBook cover photo (JPG) plus the Mobi file;

    b. For paperback books distributed on Amazon via CreateSpace or KDP, you will need the book cover file (PDF file) plus the interior formatted pages (PDF file);

    c. For non-Kindle eBooks distributed through Ingram Spark, you will need the eBook cover photo (JPG) plus the Epub file; and

    d. For all print books distributed through Ingram Spark, you will need the book cover files (PDF file for paperback and/or PDF file for hard cover) plus the interior formatted pages (the same PDF file will work for both the paperback and hard cover).

Also, you will need the following information when you upload your files:

    a. The title and subtitle of your book;

    b. The name(s) of the author(s) and illustrator(s) of your book;

    c. The publisher's name;

    d. For print books, the trim size;

e. The sales description of the book;

f. Two or three BISAC codes for your book;

g. The ISBN numbers assigned to each version of your book; and

h. Five to seven keywords or short phrases for your book.

❑ <u>STEP 13: Register your book with the U.S. Copyright Office within three months after the publication date</u>. To do this, you should:

a. Follow the instructions for the online registration form on the eCO Registration System;

b. Pay the applicable fee ($35); and

c. Mail two copies of your book to the U.S. Library of Congress after publication.

❑ <u>STEP 14: Market your book</u>. There are many ways to promote your new book. This step is never-ending and takes up as much time and money as you are willing to invest. Do your research and don't be afraid to experiment to find the marketing campaigns that work best for your book.

ABOUT THE AUTHOR

By day, Mike Kowis, Esq., is a mild-mannered tax attorney at a Fortune 500 company in Texas. By night, he swaps a three-piece suit for a pair of tights and a shiny red cape and then begins his duties as a modern-day SUPERHERO (a.k.a. "Adjunct Faculty Member") for one of the largest community colleges in the Lone Star State. His superpower is ENGAGING COLLEGE STUDENTS in Business Law and Corporate Tax classes. He has spent the past 15 years fearlessly fighting for truth, justice, and the American way! Well, not really. But he did spend that time trying to fully engage his college students in night classes, which is just as hard.

In his award-winning debut book, *Engaging College Students: A Fun and Edgy Guide for Professors*, Mike shared the secrets to his success in the college classroom. Specifically, he provided 44 college teaching tips to help any teacher create a fun and lively learning environment, engage students in thought-provoking classroom discussions, motivate them to read the assigned materials, inspire them to attend all classes and stay till the final bell rings, and encourage them to use their critical thinking skills.

In this book, *14 Steps to Self-Publishing a Book*, Mike explains in great detail how he turned the manuscript of his first book into a high-quality self-published book. He spells out the 14 steps that anyone can take to self-publish a top quality book and sell it on websites like Amazon and BarnesandNoble.com. He also details the costs of his self-publishing journey and shares the top ten lessons he learned from writing his first book.

If you have any questions or comments about this book or would like Mike to speak at an event, please email him at mike.kowis.esq@gmail.com, find his author page on Facebook (Mike Kowis, Esq.), or visit his website at www.engagingcollegestudents.com.

Made in the USA
Columbia, SC
25 August 2018